Let's Read About . . .
Betsy Ross

For my grandmother, a truly strong woman

—D.D.

To Clarence and Ellen

—R.G.

The editors would like to thank Lori Dillard Rech,
Executive Director of the Betsy Ross House,
for her expertise.

ISBN 0-439-56635-5

Text copyright © 2004 by Danielle Denega.
Illustrations copyright © 2004 by Renee Graeff.
All rights reserved. Published by Scholastic Inc.
SCHOLASTIC, CARTWHEEL BOOKS, and associated logos are trademarks and/or registered trademarks of Scholastic Inc.

12 11 10 9 8 7 6 5 4 3 2 1   4 5 6 7 8 9/0

Printed in the U.S.A.
First printing, February 2004

Let's Read About . . .
Betsy Ross

by Danielle Denega
Illustrated by Renee Graef

SCHOLASTIC INC.
New York   Toronto   London   Auckland   Sydney
Mexico City   New Delhi   Hong Kong   Buenos Aires

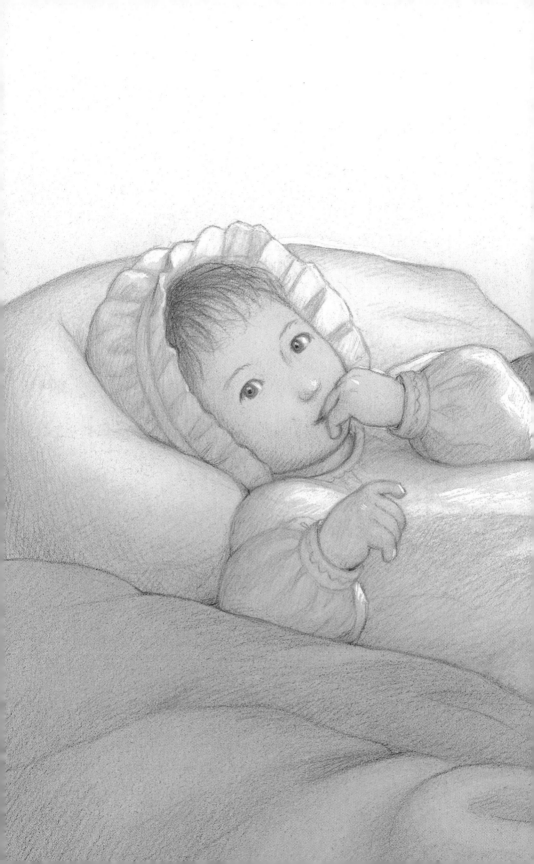

Elizabeth Griscom was born
on January 1, 1752,
in Philadelphia, Pennsylvania.
Her parents called her Betsy.
Today, she is known as Betsy Ross.

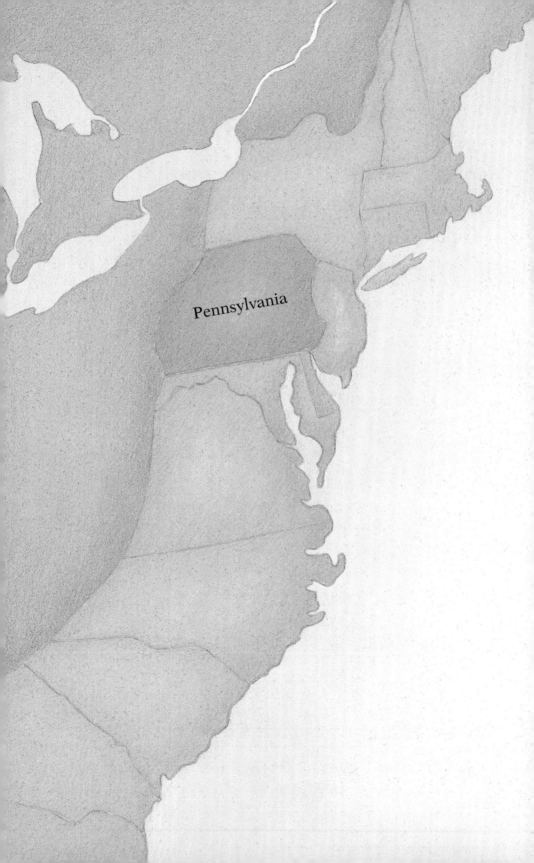

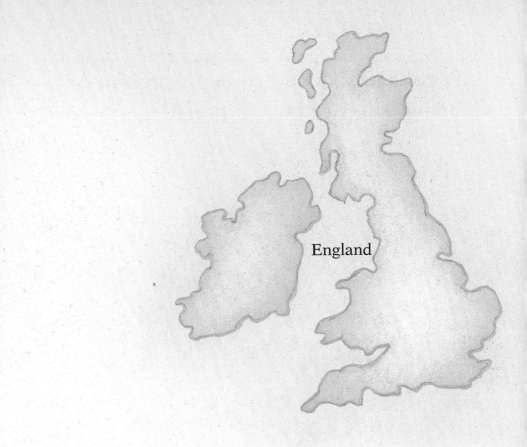

England

There was no United States of America
at that time.
Pennsylvania was one
of the thirteen colonies.
The colonies belonged to the country
of England.

Betsy had sixteen brothers and sisters!
She was a very busy little girl.

She helped take care of her younger
brothers and sisters.
She did many of the chores.

Betsy, her mother, and her sisters
made clothes for the whole family.
Betsy became very good at sewing.

Not many girls went to school
in colonial times.
Boys would go.

Girls stayed at home
to do chores.
But Betsy was lucky enough
to go to school!
She learned to read, write, and
do math.
She learned to sew even better.

Betsy stopped going to school
when she was twelve years old.
She took a job at a shop.
Here, Betsy sewed tablecloths, curtains,
and bedspreads.

Betsy was one of the best workers
at the shop.
A young man named John Ross worked
at the sewing shop, too.

They became good friends.
Then they got married.
Betsy's last name became Ross.

Betsy and John opened their own
shop in 1775.
The thirteen colonies were trying
to break free from England at that time.

Many colonists did not want to listen
to the King of England anymore.
They wanted to be in charge
of the colonies themselves.
Betsy and John believed in this, too.

The thirteen colonies went to war
with England.
The war was called the American
Revolution.
John became a soldier.
He died in an accident during the war.

Betsy was alone now.
She decided to keep the shop open.
She ran it by herself.

Betsy sewed clothes for the soldiers
to make extra money.
She even sewed shirts for
General George Washington.

George Washington was the leader
of the colonists during the war.
He later became the first President
of the United States.

Here is the legend of Betsy Ross
and the American flag:
In the spring of 1776,
George Washington came to
Betsy's shop.

He wanted Betsy to make a very
special flag.
It might become the flag
of the new colonies.

Betsy had ideas about
how the flag should look.
She made the flag a rectangle shape.
She put five-pointed stars on it.

George Washington liked Betsy's flag.

The flag was going to fly
from the ships fighting in the war.

Betsy's flag flew high from these ships.

The British gave up in October of 1781.
The colonies had won their freedom.

Our flag got 13 stars and 13 stripes on June 14, 1777.
It was the flag of the new United States of America.

June 14 is still celebrated as Flag Day
all across the country.
The American flag now has fifty stars —
one for each state.
It still has thirteen stripes — one for
each of the original colonies.